The Air Around Us

by

Christopher Hivner

ISBN: 978-81-19228-56-0

First Edition: 2023
Rs. 200/-

Cyberwit.net
HIG 45 Kaushambi Kunj, Kalindipuram
Allahabad - 211011 (U.P.) India
http://www.cyberwit.net
Tel: +(91) 9415091004
E-mail: info@cyberwit.net

Printed at Vcore.

Contents

Yesterday Afternoon

She listened to the music
for an escape.
The singer searched
for a "heart of gold",
a harmonica blaring
in her ears.
A bitter laugh
broke from her tongue
to consume the air
around her.
"There's no such thing,"
she said to her living room
as she stared out
the window
at a cloudless sky,
a new day
to replace
yesterday afternoon
and her father's nonchalance
while ruining her world.
How dare the sky
shine so blue
she thought.
The revelations she heard
should cover the world
in ash
so she's not alone
in her haze.
The air she breathed

on this day after
choked her lungs
and the image
of her former hero
melted before her
leaving soiled bone,
the teeth still chattering
his confession that
“he needed to make
before I die.”

The music stopped,
the singer’s search over.
She tried to rise
from the couch
but her legs refused
and her heart
had no fight.
Her eyes remained
on the perfect
summer sky
while her mind
conjured photos
of all the women
her father had cheated with,
printed pictures
pinned in the air
flapping in the wind
like they were waving to her,
mouths open
to regale her
with the tawdry details:
“Your dad did me

every Thursday for a decade."
"It was just once
when he was supposed
to be at your soccer game."
"I'm sure your mom knew about us,
we weren't shy."
"We started before he got married
and couldn't stop."

The hours finally relented
bringing night to her door
so the sky
turned as black
as her mood.
She had her laptop open
skimming photos of her parents
joined at the hip,
smiling,
her father like a reptile
and mother like a saint
she now thought.
It was all too much,
the way he had shifted
his burden to her
pinning it to her breast
for all to see,
I am the daughter
of a bad man.
She slammed the laptop shut.

The silence
led her through the night
to eventual fitful sleep.

She woke
to day two
of her new reality,
day two of
mining for forgiveness
in an empty vein.
Another blue sky
welcomed her,
mocked her,
but she moved forward.
A trip was planned
to her mother's grave.
They had a lot
to talk about.

The Green-Eyed Girl

The green-eyed girl
hung back
a few feet from the table
at the flea market.
Customers buzzed around,
busy, busy, busy lives
keeping them self-centered,
not even noticing
when they bumped into
one another.
Orders were spit out,
money shook
by greedy hands.
Give me what I want,
give it to me now.
Credit cards waved
like a king's or queen's scepter,
meet my demands
quickly and with respect.
The young girl,
part of the family,
owners, workers, bakers,
was supposed to be
waiting on customers,
but she just stared,
her eyes wide with tension,
her mind
gamboling through the pages
of her drawing notebook,

beautiful worlds
covered in mist,
populated by creatures
she birthed.
She was back in the forest
of 1000-foot-high trees,
a new life form
she had just thought of
climbing the silver limbs
of the oldest tree.
The green-eyed girl
wasn't where she wanted to be.
The faces before her
demanded attention,
but everything inside of her
belonged to her creations,
with some left over
for her family,
she didn't care
how many donuts
the man in the blue hat wanted.
Yes, we have apple pies,
but she didn't want to give one
to the belching woman
in the too small dress.
The money they
shoved at her
meant nothing.
The sun pounded down
on her face,
the customers' bodies
pressed too close.
Her family bustled about her

selling, selling, selling . . .
and the trees
reached for her,
limb-arms pulling her
deeper into the forest,
her creations
took her hand
to lead her
into this sanctuary,
to make it hers.
The mist surrounded
the green-eyed girl
until she was gone,
bathed only
in her own light.

Antimatter

I'm told my father attended
my high school graduation.
I couldn't prove it
because he left
as soon as the ceremony ended,
never spoke to me.
At my wedding
he waved to me
from the back of the church
and in the line after
said "congratulations".
One word.
Left the reception
as we arrived.
We were like
matter and antimatter,
couldn't exist
in the same space
at the same time.
He paid for
my first car
but I still didn't see him.
He gave the money
to my older brother
who bought the car.
I think about
the times I did
see/speak to him,
not exactly how

you're supposed to remember
dear old dad.
Mom asked him, told him,
begged him
to see me, talk to me,
acknowledge my existence,
but he didn't or couldn't
or didn't care,
take your pick.
I've been told
many things
about my father,
seen the photos,
hung them on my wall,
but the effect is the same,
father and son
still not in the same place
at the same time.

When I Left the House

I took one last look around
at the empty rooms
that had once held us
in the form of
art on the wall,
furniture picked out
on a blustery Saturday afternoon
and ephemera
bought on a whim.

The air in the house
that was no longer ours
entered my lungs
with a stale bite
as I walked
from room to room,
telling myself
I was making sure
nothing was left behind,
but it was a wistful
trip back in time
to where I no longer belonged.

I was reluctant to leave.
I stood on the steps
to the landing
staring into the empty living room
as ghosts danced
over the carpeting

we had installed
a month after moving in.
The spirits didn't acknowledge me,
and I didn't want
to let them go.

I pulled the door shut,
hearing the familiar click
of the lock,
stood on the cement slab
that was the porch
holding onto the doorknob.
When I finally released it,
something swept over me
but it was too soon
to discern whether
it was relief, trepidation,
or confusion.

I walked to my car
and got in,
hesitating one last time.
I didn't look at the house
but at the snow that was
starting to fall.
I waited until
my front window
was covered,
obscuring the house,
the neighborhood,
and our once
home street,
took a deep breath

that caught in my throat
before starting the car,
turned on the wipers
and drove away.

The Actress

She ate it all, every bite,
as though it were haute cuisine,
suckling meat roasted by God
with fresh vegetables
from his personal garden
and a cup of coffee
percolated from beans
shit out by a beast
straight from Eden.
Her performance was magnificent,
turning every bite
of Salisbury steak
and frozen broccoli
into theater of the absurd,
but they bought it.
They always bought it
from her,
she'd spent a lifetime
fooling everyone.

When she was finished,
they pushed her back to her room
where her world resided,
smelling of disinfectant
and decaying flesh.
The void absorbed her like a sponge
and she was alone,
lying in bed
staring at pictures of a dead husband
and two children

who played the ghost,
emerging from the ether
once or twice a year
to pat her head,
hold her hand
and glance at their watches.
She would consume it all
and hold it tight in her belly
while smiling broadly,
telling stories that never happened,
reminiscing about love
that never existed,
acting her age and infirmity
until they left,
relieved of duty.
She could fool them
in her sleep
she could fool them all.

If the woman in the other bed
would stop moaning,
if the man down the hall
would stop yelling for Jesus,
she could sleep at night,
but if she slept
she would dream
and then she would hate herself even more
than she already does.
They all appeared when she dreamt,
every decision she ever made,
every desire she let out in the sun
to dry up
like a worm,
every apology she accepted

when she was as angry as a snake,
every compromise she brokered
that left her with nothing,
like zombies
they crawled
from the crevasses of her brain
to eat what was left
of her decrepit form
and her smiles
wouldn't satiate them.

She can fool the living,
but not the memories.
They know her secrets,
roasting them on a spit
until they crackle
and gleam with juices,
gathering around the campfire
to swap tales
of eighty-three.years of
unrequited romance,
self-sacrifice
and timid bones.
When morning came
she would be tired,
but grinning,
holding her bowels
while intoning good morning
to the nurses
and sundry life around her.
They all loved her
because she never gave anyone
any trouble.

He Fought

He fought for his country
surrounded by Japanese water
assuming he would die
and never have a life
that didn't include jungles, malaria
and death reaching for him
in the guise of a bullet.

He fought with himself
for control. The jungles had been nothing
compared to a wife and kids
when there were so many other ladies
that needed love
or at least a good screw.

He fought with his girlfriend,
she called the house.
He felt like one of the bullets
had finally found him.
Open warfare and a kamikaze flying low,
crashing through the door.

He fought with himself,
for right and wrong.
The kids would understand, the wife would understand.
He fought for his freedom,
now he had to have it,
and he would be back every so often
for some home cookin',
wink and a smile.

He fought with his wife,
walk out the door and he couldn't come back.
Life didn't work that way,
malaria or no,
veteran or no,
right or wrong
and he was gone.

He fought for his country
and helped win our freedom.
He fought with himself
and lost his way
down a path
that ended in the jungle.

The Art of Letting Go

I sit on the beach
to watch the waves
and listen to the soothing sound
of the water crashing to shore.
If not for the sun
melting my skin
I could have fallen
into a deep sleep.
A young couple walked past.
She was tall, graceful,
walking, even through the sand,
with a confident carriage.
The boy was short, stout,
stepping heavily,
with his left arm
wrapped tightly around his girl's waist,
hanging on for dear life,
waiting for her
to escape
into the arms of another.
If he could have encased her
in both arms
and still been able to walk
I believe he would have.
It made me retreat to years past
when I used to have someone
to walk the beach with,
we didn't tether ourselves
to one another,

just held hands,
a safe,
but easily breakable bond,
not sure of who we were
or who we belonged to.
Now I wondered,
should we have strangled
each other
with affection,
to own those moments
and one another?
Later, I saw the couple again,
laughing and smiling,
this time holding hands.
I turned my attention
back to the waves.

Beyond the Sunset

I was thinking
about that one time
you picked me up
at the train station
and stared at me dreamily
the whole drive home.
I'd been gone for three days,
your soft eyes, genuine smile,
made it seem like
I'd come home from the war
and not Atlanta.
Thirty varied years
have passed
but I still remember
your look, your demeanor,
your eyes lit me
like a Klieg light,
you held my hand
with the strength
of desperation.
I felt loved in a way
I didn't know existed,
elevated to a pedestal
I never could have climbed
on my own.
The glow kept me warm,
the heat sparked nerves under my skin
and I rode my high horse
into the desert

the long hair of my youth
flowing behind me
a soft acoustic guitar
playing me off
beyond the sunset.

Afternoon Sky

A name popped
into my head,
someone I haven't
talked to
in years.

He used to be
a friend
but time
and distance
have rendered us
to nothing.

There were days
when we laughed
and others
where talk led
to philosophy
or history,
the past and
its mysteries.

Our paths diverged
leading us away,
slowly at first,
but eventually
like trains
behind schedule.

Now when his face
appears in my mind
I indulge the memories
for a bit,
not too long
because time
has pulled us apart
like clouds
for a reason.
You can't return
to a singular moment,
not with the same energy,
the same verve,
the same result.

The name of someone
I hadn't seen
in years
crossed my mind
and I let him
drift away
against the
afternoon sky.

Maybe Tomorrow

The neighbor's dogs
just kept barking,
invading the silence
of his house.
A silence he needed
to prop up his bones
before he slid away
down the kitchen drain.

Lying on the couch
in a Friday afternoon stupor
he waved goodbye
to another week wasted,
another chapter of his life
that would bore the readers
of the life story
he will never write.

Ah, there it was,
glorious quiet.
The mongrels have been
taken inside.
Now he could do
important thinking
about why his mother
left when he was ten,
why his relationships
never worked out,
why his dog died young.

Why no one ever
gave him a cool nickname.
Where did his
old baseball cards go
and why didn't Mom
ever come back.

These and many other questions
will never be answered
on today's edition
of couch thoughts
followed soon after
by light up sundown,
one man, one joint, one lighter.

1995 is when she left,
wearing her too big winter coat
because she was always cold,
mouthful of Ibuprofen
to cure her never ending headache
and a cigarette dangling from her lips,
she couldn't quit,
she was under too much stress
but leaving her ten-year-old son
would fix everything.

"I'm sorry, I have to go,"
were her last words
before the door shut,
Dad wasn't even
home from work yet
which left him alone,
staring at the back

of a wood paneled door,
listening to her POS Cavalier
spit and choke
as she backed out of the driveway.

The couch on Friday night
would provide no answers
just as his mother
never could either
since she died
eight years after she left,
in a car accident
riding with her
alcoholic boyfriend
who didn't stress her
like a ten-year-old boy did.

He wanted the dogs
to bark again,
anything to drown out
the air slowly leaking
from his body.
He sat up,
willing himself to move,
to plug the leak.
Maybe tomorrow
he'd figure it all out.
Maybe tomorrow
he would let go.

Proof

She turned the car engine off
and laid her head
against the seat's headrest.
It was after midnight,
she was tired,
the weight
of what he was doing
pulled her skin down
until it dragged behind her
as she walked.
It was time
to get proof
so she could . . .,
well, do *something*.
The other woman's house
stared back at her,
the heavy-lidded windows
glaring with contempt,
the front door panels
were four wide mouths
laughing at her.
"Why are you here?"
they asked,
"You can't change him,
only yourself."
She fingered the necklace
she wore.
"I need to see him,"
she said softly.

"I need it to be real
so that I can breathe again."
The house shuddered
with shame
and asked no more questions
of her.

Almost 1:30 a.m.,
she nearly nodded off.
Her finger was on
the car's start button.
It was time
to go home
and decide
to either keep living
wrapped in the
cloth of his lies
or confront him,
make him
flay her flesh
with his confession.
She pressed the button,
and her car started.
She hadn't stopped
staring at the house door,
and now it swung open,
the four mouths
swallowing her
into the house's belly.
She felt like throwing up,
but her tongue
held it in,

Her husband
made his appearance
at 1:36 a.m.,
stepping onto the top step
with the bravado
of a movie star,
looking around
like he expected paparazzi.
Her breath caught
in her throat
when he turned around
and pulled
his whore
close to him
for one last kiss
and squeeze of ass.
So, there it was,
proof.
Her husband of nine years
was cheating on her,
selling his affections
for a suck and a lay,
selling their marriage
a minute at a time.

She had
what she came for
so why couldn't
she move?
The car's engine
idled softly,
the meditative music
from the stereo

swept around her
like gentle Caribbean waves,
she was in
a cocoon,
but still
felt like she was bleeding
from the sliced glass
of his tongue.

She wanted to scream,
or laugh, anything,
but she was immobilized
by it all,
her fears, his adultery,
the world spinning on
no matter
who was right
or who was wrong,
she didn't win either way.
Tears wanted to spill,
but she wouldn't let them.
It would be
giving him another piece
he didn't deserve.
She clenched her jaw,
willed him to get
to his car
and drive away.

And then
she was alone,
the soft leather
of her car seat

holding her,
the music
embracing ger gently,
the darkness,
for the first time,
easing her fears.
It was time
to find a new home.

The Air Around Us

I was only happy
when I was
inside you,
fleeting minutes
ticking by
when we were
connected as one
and then it ended,
the air around us,
once warm,
crackling with energy,
now pulled away
from us
as if it knew
the rest of
our togetherness
was a fraud.
I never breathed well after,
and your eyes
lost color,
our voices
spoke in half sentences,
touches only moments ago sensual,
now perfunctory
as if it was a procedure
to be followed.
When we were one,
stars danced over
our heads

and the air was thick
around us
like a cocoon.
And when it was over,
our energy sapped,
the sheen of sweat
oiling our skin,
we slowly pulled apart,
tasting copper
on our tongues,
lying next to love
instead of
existing inside of it.

Set List

They encountered the gunman
    in the hallway
    as they walked to their room,
    laughing at Cindy's joke,
    discussing what songs
    they hoped to hear
    at the concert later that night.
    He nodded at the pretty girls
    as he walked past,
    they didn't notice him.
They encountered the gunman
    outside while Dave
    had a smoke
    and snorted his way
    through a story
    about the flight in
    and the woman who
    got stuck in the bathroom.
    They didn't realize
    the man in the gray baseball cap
    was listening and laughing along.
They encountered the gunman
    in the parking lot
    using a broken metal coat hanger
    to get into a Dodge van.
    The young policemen
    checked his license and registration
    and they could see the keys
    dangling from the ignition.

The officers used
their own slim jim
to assist,
leaving without finding
the guns and ammunition
hidden in the back.
They encountered the gunman
at 9:16 p.m.
during the band's second song
when the bullets
made in his basement
ripped through their flesh.
They fell to the ground,
the strum of the guitar
still in their ears,
the beat of the drums
still rumbling through their chest.
They encountered the gunman
on a night filled with excitement,
anticipation, music
and community,
when the stars in the sky
made promises
to lifelong friends
and newly met lovers
that were sealed
by 10,000 voices
singing in unison
to a song that felt
written just for them.
They encountered the gunman
under a three quarters full moon
on the worst night of his life

when all the collected anger
exploded from his heart
into a statement
no one will hear
over the sound of the screams.

Wretched

I lied to my father
that morning
because the truth
was wretched.
Our first conversation
in a thousand days
and I started
with a plea
for help
to keep me
out of jail.
I needed him
to not see me
in that hour
just like
during all the years
already buried,
so I could
hold my humiliation
close
like a holy vestment.
I lied
through the
acid in my throat
into a
pair of eyes
that didn't care
one way or
the other.

I had looked into
those eyes
when he said goodbye
in my childhood,
leaving for a long trip
he said,
that turned out
to be
across town
to plant his flag
in another woman.
I had waited
by my window
for his return,
but Jezebel
kept her legs coiled
around his mid-section
convulsing in rhythm
to his indifference.

To those eyes
I was the
family dog
that needed put out of
my misery,
this wasn't
a man's son,
I stood before him
a coward,
losing at everything
because I couldn't
forgive him,
and now I couldn't

tell the truth
because I had made
him important,
more meaningful
than the sun and the moon
and the gravity
that held me
in his orbit.

I don't know
what he saw
in those jungles
in '44,
never confided in me
his thoughts
on anything,
but on dark nights
when the roads
are quiet
and I feel him
in my blood
we search together
for the sacristy
with the secret
to make us whole.
I have to
find it soon
because I'm so tired.

I lied to my father
because the truth
wouldn't make
a difference

between us.
He saw me
that day
the same as
any other,
a whisper
from his past,
a breeze
that crossed his skin
when the alcohol
was low
in his veins
and the whore
slept peacefully
next to him,
his own eyes
kept open
by his beating heart.

S.O.S

God is trying to tell me something,
I can feel it
in the blood
pumping through
my wobbly heart.
A message is being sent
over waves
I can't connect to.
"Hello?"
I shout into
the empty room
waiting for a booming voice
to crack my skull.

I listen.
I listen.
I look around the room.
I look around the universe
between the points of light
in the velveteen sky.
I look into the mirror.
I close my eyes
to the surrounding everything,
exist only in the quiet moment,
I scream into the gloom.

God is trying to tell me something,
I can feel it
in the twitch

of my angry nerves.
A message is being sent,
something alive and bustling.
It's here,
under my skin,
asking for a response,
just like it has
a thousand times before.

The Lonely Hours

I had a dream last night.
I was walking through a town
that wasn't mine,
down brick-home lined streets,
people sputtering this way and that,
children playing,
parents smoking,
life proceeding on its axis.
It was late
when I came upon
a young man with a round face
wearing thick glasses
making a bomb.
I watched as he set it off perfunctorily
and his friends nodded
their approval.
Then he built a larger version,
packing it with
nine inch nails
handed to him by his mother.
a group of sullen old men
walked up and stood too close.
They quietly asked to buy some of the nails
for a purpose they kept hidden.
The round faced kid kept working, replying,
"Don't have any nails."
The old men grumbled
"We can see them."
"You're wrong," was the answer they received.

This group,
that moved together
like a school of fish
shuffled away mumbling,
betraying themselves as
people who were used
to not getting what they wanted.
The bomb maker
set off his creation,
the report from the explosives
rocking the early morning,
setting the sky on fire.
His friends laughed hard
and cheered drunkenly.
The bomb maker's face
remained passive
as if he couldn't decide
whether what he'd done
was good
or just necessary.
I retraced my path toward home,
eventually seeing the sun come up.
While I absent-mindedly
stared at the orange-streaked horizon
I almost walked into the road.
Two cars,
traveling in opposite directions,
both stopped,
kindly waving for me to cross.
I continued my walk
thinking of all I had seen
through the lonely hours,
waking before I reached home.

We Remain

Like a movie
it plays in my head,
the old reel
flicking and chattering,
the images bouncing
with lines running through the center
and hairs wiggling
in the corners.
My brain
keeps flicking the rewind button
and then start
to run it again.
The setting never changes,
the words are the same,
sepia tone faces
lined with tears
and the ending comes
same as before.
He's gone
and we remain.
Run it back again
my brain demands
but I can't
anymore tonight.
I force the projector off,
the film flips, flips, flips
to a stop.
He's gone,
we remain.

Chance and Choice

In the picture
five men in an awkward row,
two I know,
but not as well
as I should.
Both were gone
before I was three feet tall,
one taken by illness,
the other
wanderlust.
I look in their eyes
caught on film
decades ago
and try to read
their thoughts.
I wonder
what it would
have been like
to know them better,
Grandpa and Dad,
left me behind
by chance
and by choice.
The photo is them
on a bowling team.
Could I have been
on a team
with them
when I was older?

Would they
have taught me
to drive,
to believe in myself,
to talk to girls,
to fix the toilet
or build a shed.
Their eyes
from an ancient photo
can't give me
any answers,
so why do I
keep trying?
Because they are me,
I carry their blood
under my skin,
their traits
in my genes,
their mysteries
in my enigmas.
By chance or by choice
I want to know them.

On Through the Night

Driving across the bridge,
one hand on the wheel
the other resting
against the window,
his index finger
wiping at the condensation
building on the glass,
the man who was lost
couldn't remember
where he was driving to.
His mind,
once swirling with thoughts,
was now a gray spot,
dense with regrets,
unfulfilled dreams
and anxiety
so deep
he gave it a name
(The Captain)
and talked to it
when the night
crawled over his skin
with the tickling feet
of a centipede.

The rain outside
tapped on the windshield
while he drove,
welcoming him to

the way things are,
a land of
doubt and inactivity
because as The Captain says,
if you do nothing
you're safe,
if you make the
wrong decision,
you're fucked.
The rain
was an old friend,
comfort found
in the soft noise
and inevitability
of the next drop
and the next and
the next . . .

The man who was lost
exited the highway
across the bridge,
to tamer
back country roads,
bends and curves
where deer
cross in the darkness
and farmhouses
appear out of the fog
like apparitions.
Where was he going?
Nowhere in particular,
just driving
because he didn't want

to be sitting
at home.
The hypnotic thump
of the wipers,
the steady gear-changing
of the engine,
the tick-tick-tick
of his turn signal,
all of it calmed
his troubled heart.

The next right turn
took him toward home
and when he realized,
he flinched.
The embryo of
his emptiness
was formed there.
It was getting late,
he was tired,
home called
out of duty,
the solid, stale house
wrapping him in
arms of silence.
The man who was lost
didn't know where
to go,
but he wasn't going home.

On through the night
he drove,
through small towns,

over bridges,
under overpasses,
past farms, hospitals
and housing developments.
This man
who once
had a family,
commanded respect,
and had a structured
daily life,
now didn't know
where he was going
and had
nowhere to go
as The Captain steered him
with fearful hands.
The rain continued falling,
he drove through
the downpour
to find the morning.

Saturdays

Afternoons, at first

me bowling alone
Dad keeping score,
telling me to get more loft on the ball

Afternoons, later

me playing alone in Dad's house
Dad in the easy chair
watching bowling on tv

Afternoon, the last day

me at home alone, waiting
for Dad's car to pull up
Dad asleep on the couch at his house

Outside the Window

I had a dream
where we walked hand in hand
down a path
cut through a cornfield,
our free hands tapping the cobs
along the way.
The placidity of the hours
raised the joy
on our skin.
The dream went on and on,
no variation,
like a looped ten-second movie,
two hands entwined,
two others keeping contact
with the stalks.
Eventually I knew I was dreaming
and tried to wake up,
but we just kept walking,
a light wind
ruffling our clothes.
Our genuine smiles
slowly turned to plastic fakeness,
I gripped your hand harder,
I wanted to wake up,
screamed with a sleeping voice.
The path was endless
and the cornstalks seemed
to be growing taller . . .

The dog barked,
time to go out.
I sat up,
finally awake.
The dog looked at me
and ran out of the room,
I looked at you,
you back to me
as it had been
for almost a year,
outside the bedroom window
the corn grew higher
each day.

Clockwork Hearts

I drove through the night
with her asleep
in the back seat
dreaming of the color blue
and all the places
she wanted to go.
I was tired too,
but we had to keep moving
to stay together.
When we stopped
to talk
or feel anything,
our differences
rose from the hollows inside
to consume us.
Keep moving,
one adventure to another,
day after day,
night after night,
we need to stay alive
or we'll be alone.

The sun paints the first layer
of orange on the sky
just above the horizon
as I gas up the car
at a mini market
off the highway.
She's stretching

outside the woman's room
searching for her new day persona.
She drives in the rising sun
while I sleep
before we find
the fun
or the mundane,
whichever presents itself first.
Doesn't matter
as long as we
stick together
and smile to smile
move through another
twenty-four hours.

From the back seat
I see her hair flow
down her shoulders
like a waterfall.
I eventually fall asleep
despite her singing along
with every song
on the Counting Crows CD,
getting enough words right
that it became
a lullaby.
My own dreams
veer toward people
I haven't talked to
in twenty years
trying to send me a message
I can't understand,
or mom
just saying hi.

Her gentle laugh
while we stroke the goats
at a petting zoo
buried in the Delaware Valley
is what keeps me going.
That's when she's happy,
it's when we connect,
telling stories
from our childhoods,
sparks from our eyes
pulling us closer.
This is when we laugh
all day,
hold hands
like we were ten
and pretending to be adults.
These days the world
seems to like us,
the sun winks,
the clouds spell out our names.
When night approaches
on these days
we rent a motel room
to shower
and make love
for hours
before sleep overtakes us.
We fall unconscious
in each other's arms,
I'm happier than I've ever been,
but lurking
beyond my closed eyes
is the realization

I have no idea
what tomorrow
will bring.

I was thirteen
the first time I thought about
having a girlfriend,
it was all kissing
and touching,
no talking or doing anything
in particular,
only being close,
the warmth of our bodies
gluing us together.
When she was thirteen
she had a boyfriend,
not her first.
It doesn't matter
who I am with her,
I'm in a line of succession
and we are all
endlessly compared,
studied and scrutinized.
I can't win,
only lose,
I can't be
the best thing
that's ever happened to her
because there have been
too many
worst things
and now
we are all the same.

Crossing state lines
into Virginia,
good day number two in a row.
We are both well rested,
de-stressed and hydrated,
loose as a goose,
making fun
of each other's
mannerisms, favorite movies
and inability
to tell a joke.
Virginia has in store for us
an antique shop
and Chinese food for lunch.
We are together
and alive,
slowed down to enjoy
our company,
to be in love,
however fleeting
or permanent
it may turn out to be.

We live like
fugitives on the run
spending too many days
not stopping,
on the move
down the next road,
sleeping in shifts in the car
or a few hours
at shitbag motel #37
just outside of

Ditchwater, name a state.
We both dream
of permanence
but we don't trust ourselves
or each other.
I never think
about leaving her
but I believe
every day
she entertains the idea
of running away
on her own.
I won't get a goodbye
much less a reason,
I'll turn around
and she'll be gone.

We drove west,
not stopping
or talking much,
the sky appeared hard and spiteful,
like gravel,
for days.
I felt wired
because I was worried,
she slept a lot
and stared out the window
searching for an escape route.
We came apart so easily,
done in by meteorology
and familiarity.
I wouldn't give up
but was feeling the pressure
in my chest.

Staring at a wall-sized canvas
at the art institute
in Chicago
and it makes no sense.
An eight-year-old
could have painted it
so why is it
in a museum?
She likes it
but won't explain why.
I need someone to tell me
why it exists.
She likes anything
that defies logic
while I search
for an answer
that repairs the frays
around my ragged edges.

I've never had a relationship
that worked
like they're supposed to,
after too many failures
I assumed it was me,
but she's never had one either.
One night,
looking at our reflection
in the bathroom mirror together
in a Super 8 off the highway,
she told me
ours was the best she'd had
while she looked at me
in a way

that melted my internal organs
and left me quivering.
Now I know
there is no truth.
If our abstract drifting
through our numbered days
is the best we can do,
then our misfiring wires
will eventually combust
and burn the mother down.

She turns us south
for no reason.
We haven't had fun
since Chicago.
I think we should have stayed,
at least for a week,
but her clock
said move.
My weariness that started
in my limbs
has deepened,
finding my every thought,
glazing my breaths
with the flavor
of salt.

As we move on
she's not talking to me.
I said something,
don't remember what,
and of course
she won't tell me,

so I drive in silence,
alone except for
her deep sighs.
There won't be any
motel room sex tonight.
I'll be driving
for hours
stopping only for gas
and a bathroom.
I sneak looks
in the rearview mirror
into the back seat
where she sits,
arms crossed,
tossing her head
left, then right,
searching for the correct stance
to show her irritation.
The whole show
has gotten old
so I don't buy a ticket anymore
which makes her
even more annoyed.
That makes me smile
in a stupid way.

I'm feeling detached,
like our stitching is ripping.
Part of me
is desperate to find
a seamstress
and another me
wants to let it happen.

I don't know
which state we're in.
Everything has looked the same
for miles
and she has barely
spoken to me for days.
This afternoon,
after lunch
at a diner
with the best
toasted cheese sandwich
I've ever had,
she's sitting in the passenger seat.
The distance between us
day after day
can only be measured
in the looks she gives me
where her eyes
see something,
or someone, else.
Fifty hours
after the fact
she reminded me
of what I said
that pissed her off.
My look back to her
wasn't shattered enough
and I didn't mumble
an apology
this time
because fuck that.
Her hair was frizzy
that morning,

that's all I said,
with a smile and affection
and it was taken
like a bullet to the chest.
If that's what
makes our clockwork hearts stop
then so be it,
I'm tired.

Once, she said she needed me
and that it scared her,
but it was bullshit,
she doesn't need me.
At times
she desires me,
she likes my sense of humor
and being held
while we watch a movie.
When she needs help
she likes that I'm there
because too many
haven't been.
But that doesn't translate
into need.
I'm only now realizing
I want to be needed
and she's incapable
of that verity.

I slept in the back seat
while she drove us
through Iowa.
My dreams

left me cold,
nonsense wrapped in dread,
the confusion when I woke
worse than being under.
Then I heard the quiet
in the car.
She didn't have any music playing,
no singing along with the Beatles,
no mumbling under her breath
about me
or any of her exes,
no working out
her plans for the future
in free form jazz speak
while her hands
drew diagrams in the air.
I snuck a look
as she sat rigid
in the driver's seat,
staring forward like a zombie,
hands clenching the wheel
at 10 and 2.
I turned over
to go back to sleep
but thought only of
rushing water.

Nebraska welcomed us
in the dark
and near-exhaustion.
We found a room
in a one-star motel,
had perfunctory sex

and then ate cheese popcorn
viewing a watch repairman
on a local cable access channel.
We were asleep
before the pocket watch
was ticking again,
not moving for ten hours.
The next morning
she went for a walk
and after three hours
I assumed she wasn't coming back,
but then the door opened.
She casually told me
she had booked the room
for another night.
Then she laid down
and took a nap.
I watched her sleep
for awhile
but there was
no air in the room.
I felt a change
so deep inside
my bones hurt.
I stared out the window
at a desultory parking lot
and every time
I saw a car pull out
I felt the tug
I never had before.
I knew the time
would come
but didn't expect it to be me

that chose the minute.
I stroked her hair lightly,
kissed two of my fingertips
and placed them
to her cheek
before turning out the light
and leaving the room.

The car was hers
so I walked across the street
to a truck stop diner,
got a meal to go
and met Donny,
a long-haul driver
who agreed to give me a ride
as far as his final stop.
When we pulled out
in Donny's rig
I didn't look back.
The line between us
that had kept our bodies touching
and our hearts beating
had been severed
for no good reason,
but then again,
we had connected
the same way.

Good Night, Andre Agassi

I rode home
on the train
from the city,
my visit a short one,
just enough
to remind me
of past dalliances.
The sway of the train
put me to sleep,
and I dreamed of Mom,
one of our
trips to the US Open,
Andre Agassi
gave her a wink
as he hit the match winner
and Mom stood and clapped
until I woke up
listening to another
unintelligible announcement
of the next stop
on the Keystone line.

Mom tried to get
Agassi's autograph once
as he came off
the practice courts,
but he was surrounded
by security
and a throng of fans.

Mom being 70 years old
and five feet
plus a pinch,
she never had a chance.

The train pulled into Philly
where it stopped
for thirty minutes.
I watched
groups of people excitedly
leave the train
to go into
the station
for drink and food,
running like
it was their birthday,
and the Starbucks
at 30th street station
had a cake
waiting for them.

Mom got other autographs
on a visor she wore,
Tommy Haas, Todd Martin,
and others I don't remember,
but Agassi
was her white whale,
always too many people,
Andre always in a hurry.

The adventurers,
red-faced with excitement,
re-board the train

holding their treasure,
Coca Cola and sandwiches
from a train station restaurant,
could life get better
than this?
I had spent my time
thinking about Mom,
she and New York
inextricably linked
in my mind.

The view from the train window
is sometimes urban,
at others rural,
still others industrial,
dilapidated and battle-worn.
My eyes
take it all in,
remembering the small towns
I grew up in,
so different from
much of what I see.

Mom got to see Agassi play
a few times at the US Open,
albeit from far up in
Arthur Ashe Stadiun,
closer to the clouds
than to her beloved Andre.
They were first round matches,
so the outcome
was never in doubt
but still provided Mom

the thrill of seeing
her favorite.

As we pull into
Lancaster PA,
the energy of New York
has dissipated,
replaced by the quietude
of my home,
small town
south central Pennsylvania.
I trade the sway of the train
for the mid-price luxury
of my SUV.

At home
my trip is now behind me,
memories to be accessed
in a month
or a year.
My last wave to the city
is a long distance
see you later.
Exhaustion welcomes me,
and when I am
safely in my bed
ready to sleep
I say goodnight
to Andre Agassi's
number one fan.

When You Weren't Speaking

You knew I was leaving,
so you wouldn't look at me
Or was it "but"
you wouldn't look?
Let's be honest,
you wanted me to go
but you couldn't ask me
or tell me,
straight forward wasn't your way.
I took the initiative
to give you what you wanted
while you stared at the wall
grim-faced and scheming.
It took awhile
for me to carry my stuff
to the car,
you stayed silent
the whole time
and quiet
wasn't your way either.
What were you thinking
when you weren't speaking?
I tried to read your eyes
but they showed as much
as your mouth said.
When I was finished
removing my life
from the house,
I returned your key,

sliding it across the table
where it lay
out of your sight line
because you refused
to turn your head
from the ever-fascinating wall.
I wish I'd had
whatever the wall had that day,
maybe I wouldn't have had
to leave,
maybe you would have asked me
to stay.

The Last Days of Winter

The limb
of the winter tree
jutted out at me
like spider's legs.
I stared through
the window,
snow on the ground,
teeth in the air,
I was trapped
in the belly of February.

I remembered a picture
I had of you once,
not quite smiling,
hands in your pockets
which you rarely did,
sunglasses hiding your eyes
You weren't there
even though
you were standing in front of me.
I was taking a picture
of a ghost,
haunting me
before we were even dead.

The wind blew
the tree branches
so it looked like
they were

moving toward me,
and I felt the cold
seeping through the walls.
Removing my glasses,
for a moment,
I thought I saw
a figure
standing in the doorway.
I blinked
and it was gone.

I hate that picture
but can't forget it
for the ugliness
and signals you
were sending
and I was too soft
to receive.
It was a cheap photo
that never had a chance.

The tree limbs
are so spindly
I wonder why they
frighten me
when they reach out.
I need to change clothes
into something warmer,
armor to survive
the last days of winter
like I did
with you.

Endless Clips of Ammo

Serial killer in Toronto
Two police officers shot in Colorado
Homeless men gunned down in Las Vegas
Good morning,
time to go out into a world
that waits for you
with a mouthful of fangs
and endless clips of ammo.

Five headless bodies in Mexico
13 year old girl stabbed
Football player run down by drunk driver
Walk out your front door
into a world
that hates you.
Drink your morning coffee
to stay alert
for the one that has your name.

Earthquake in Taiwan
Hurricane in Puerto Rico
Typhoon in Indonesia
Work all day with one eye
glancing over your shoulder,
speak to others
but don't say the wrong word.

Tax cuts for the rich, but not for you
Health insurance for senators, but not for you

A raise for congress, but none for you
Drive home,
comfortable in the knowledge
that no one
is going to help you.

Go to sleep
with a prayer
or an upraised middle finger,
whichever helps you cope,
knowing that during the night
the world will keep spinning
toward oblivion.

Who We Really Are

I know you like to think
you're always right
and there was a time
when I was ok going along
with your bullshit
but that time passed
like a dead animal in the road
after you sold yourself
to another man
and wrapped yourself
in the pink ribbons of lies.
The days when words
coming out of your mouth
warmed my skin
and tightened my groin
have rotted in the noonday sun,
the stench now
a callous reminder
of who you really are.
I used to think I was smart,
or at least
not stupid,
until that night
when you just wouldn't shut up
about what you'd done,
all to soothe your own guilt.
"I feel so much better"
your face seemed to say
while I melted in the moonlight.

I used to believe
in colors,
in terrifying honesty,
but not in the death of us.
So I couldn't let it happen,
I let you back in,
right through the front door,
teary eyes and remorse.
I knew.
I did it anyway,
a deep drum beat
of who I really am.

One Last Time

Sitting in the car
next to you
feeling anxious
when I should have
felt loved.
You gave me the picture
I asked for,
although reluctantly.
I don't know why
you wanted to keep a photo
when you didn't want
to keep us,
but I guess the same
could be asked of me.
Then I heard the apology
followed by excuses.
Sure, why not,
one last time
for shits and giggles.
By then
your voice was an
automated drone
on rewind and repeat
and I was almost gone,
but not in one place.
Part of me was
in the future
with someone who won't grind me down
the way you do,

and part of me
was walking from the car
back into the house
hand in hand
with you.

Days in the Past

My restive mind
fights with the
soft music
for control of
my emotions.
The low synthesizer
soothes my veins
enough for me
to lay my head down,
but once on a mountain of pillows
trenchant thoughts
spike the calm
like bullets from a sniper rifle,
pinpoint accuracy
I never see coming.
A restorative voice sings
like a lullaby
so I can close my eyes,
trying to dream
of lazy days on the river
and her tan skin
under the sun.
I can always feel
the darkness lurking though,
a blind-alley trap
to keep me insomnolent.
A piano starts from the stereo,
keys pressed with a light touch
and a heartbeat bass

behind them,
and finally
I drift away,
the current taking me back
to the days I need.

High Sun

It was warm that afternoon,
heat, humidity, desire
all pasted together,
a craft project
of you and me
fucking on a blanket
in the yard.
Good thing
your parents lived
far away from
beady eyes looking through
the bent slats of ancient blinds.
It had been a good day,
fun abounded,
finished off
with public nudity
and a carnal act
we both needed
in a place
that was familiar
but with a trace of danger
since you know who
could come home.
Even the high sun
couldn't melt our lust
for a brief hour
of our youth.
I see that moment sometimes
when I think of you,

our fractious breathing
like a dirty rock n' roll song
getting bleeped on the radio.
My body into yours,
your body into mine,
the smell of your skin
mixed with hot, summer air,
it's all like it happened yesterday
when I think of you
on that summer day
with us still in love.

The Rain Continued

He sat on the porch
listening to the rain fall
onto the roof
and the tree out front.
Mom had been gone
for exactly four weeks
and in everything
he searched for her voice
talking to him.
Somehow the rain
was a conversation
between them.
He hoped the front
lasted for days,
fat, gray clouds
filled with his mother's
soft laugh
or aphorisms
only she understood.

He had been prepared,
she was 88 after all
when she didn't wake up
in the morning.
He knew
but it still hit
like they should have
had more time.
She had gone to bed

after watching a Hallmark movie
and never woke up.
He couldn't remember
the last thing he said to her
or her to him.
How could he not remember
something like that?

The rain was steady,
more a shower
than a storm,
the pat-pat-pat of the drops
on the maple tree leaves
lulled him to calm
though he continued listening
for a message.

Mother hated rain,
he remembered her tut-tutting
every time the forecast
mentioned showers or storms.
"Give me sun," she said
to the TV weatherman,
then telling him to shush
as he detailed
the hours it would rain
and the inches we would get.

He wanted to hear her voice again,
the slight South Carolina accent
she never lost
despite living in Pennsylvania
for over fifty years,

her hiccupping laugh
every time Dad told a joke,
no matter how bad it was.
He wished he had a recording
of her talking,
saying anything,
just her voice,
maybe saying his name.

The rain continued,
slow and steady,
his conversation
with Mom.
What it meant,
if anything,
he didn't know,
but he couldn't
let it go,
wouldn't go back inside
until it stopped,
even if he had to sleep
on the porch.
He couldn't miss a word,
couldn't let it end.

So Cool

When you told me,
there was a moment
where I couldn't breathe.
It was the last thing
I imagined coming out of your mouth,
the last thing
I thought you were capable of,
and you told me
so casually.
I don't know what you were feeling
in the moment,
but you were cool,
sitting on the grass next to me.
You were cool
while I was melting,
my essence running between the blades of grass
like dirty rainwater
after a storm.
So matter-of-fact,
"I slept with someone else."
So emotionless
while everything changed for me,
colors turned,
days rotted,
nights were when I pictured you
on your back
and the bile burned my throat.
So cool,
until the next days

when you needed me
to stay
so you'd still be
the same person you were before.
You were so calm,
your face hidden by the darkness.
Did you tell me at night
so you couldn't see my reaction?
Did that allow you
to sanctify your legs in the air?
So fucking cool
while I burned.

On that Island

I remember the sun,
the same light
we got back home
but it seemed different there
on that island
at that time,
like it shone on
only us,
kept us warm,
showed the way,
a friend that gave us everything.
When we got back home
the light was duller,
no sheen or sparkle,
our bones were cold
and we wandered,
searching for our path
in the dark.
Did the sun abandon us,
or did we abandon the sun?
The whole trip
was a mirage,
shimmering celestial light
hiding the chasm
that grew between us.
We clung to each other
for those halcyon days
fearful of the truth
that we knew lurked

under the glimmering water
that lifted us
into one another's arms
all the while
waiting to consume us.
We were one there
on that island,
but two before
the plane touched down
back in our natural world.
Opening the door
to the house
my skin caught on the knob
and I slowly unraveled
coming apart as I moved
through the rooms
I found you
by following your own
trails of string,
sitting alone in the bedroom
counting on your fingers
the number of days
you could continue pretending.
I lay down next to you
to remember the sun
for those few days
on that island.

The Neighbor across the Street

I watched from my porch
as my across-the-street neighbor
mowed his lawn
and trimmed the weeds
for the second time this week.
His movements
were robotic.
The blades of grass
and thistle leaves
flew in the air
with abandon
as my neighbor
slid a foot
to the left,
then another foot to the left,
a foot to the left,
to the left.

I knew he was
keeping the place immaculate
waiting for her to return.
The wife had gone,
driven away in the family sedan
with bags in the back,
moon roof open,
her favorite John Mellencamp
blasting through the stereo.
I had been
putting out the garbage

when she drove by,
gave me the finger
and sped off.
I had glanced over
to see my neighbor
standing in his driveway
staring at her taillights.

I tried consoling him,
but he was in la-la land,
showing me
how he had finished everything
on his honey-do list
in preparation for her return.
I asked if he had
spoken to her,
he muttered something about
other forms of communication
and toddled off
to wash the windows.
Again.

The neighbor's wife
had always been a pain,
reporting perceived violations
to the township.
All of us had received visits
from an inspector
and been given a
"You're good, sorry for the inconvenience."
So then she attended
the town hall meetings
to rail against inspectors

"who don't do their GD jobs
unless you slip them a bribe."
Then she threw
a loose stack of $1 bills
at the township commissioner
and spewed,
"Here, now make everything pretty,"
before storming out,
leaving her husband to sheepishly
follow her out
holding her purse.

My wife
saw the split coming.
Over breakfast one morning,
she said the wife
would either disappear one night
or the husband
was going to strip naked
and run through the streets,
asking everyone
if they had
seen his balls.

Weeks passed
and I saw my neighbor
less and less.
I knocked once.
I heard thumping,
then a crash,
followed by a string
of curse words,
an apology,

and then silence.
He never answered
the door.

It was three months
to the day that
the wife left
when the For Sale sign
was driven into
the front yard
by a slim, fussy man
in a red blazer
who checked things off
on a clipboard
and snapped photos
on his phone.
We never saw
our neighbor across the street again.
One day his car was gone
and never returned.

A new couple moved in
a few weeks later,
younger, friendlier,
providing no indication
one of them
was going to
escape in the night,
leaving behind
a babbling husk.

North Carolina

The wind blew
with lust
atop the dune,
pelting our skin
with stings of sand
although I don't think
she noticed,
sitting with her knees
pressed to her chest,
her eyes thinking
"If I hug tightly enough
I'll be somewhere else."

I sat beside her
bored,
having explored the dune
for what it was worth.
The sun heated my face,
sand got in my eyes
and mouth
while I wondered,
how did I
become invisible?

I sat next to her,
with her,
a shadow
without form
or substance

yet I could feel
myself breathing.
I was thirsty
and wanted a soda,
words came out
of my mouth:
inquiries, pleas,
jokes, nonsense,
it didn't matter.
I was already
a ghost.

It would be some time,
years in fact,
until we were separate.
There were talks,
arguments, tears,
stretches for understanding,
bitterness replaced by acceptance
replaced by bitterness.
Eventually there were people to talk to,
papers to sign
and lives to get on with.

I wore confusion
like a hat
for awhile
and never saw it
until years has passed,
when clarity suddenly
became easy.
For all the moments
that are my past,

my life changed
on a sand dune
in North Carolina
when I became
a ghost.

The Trees

We planted the trees
to watch them grow
over our years
but we saw
only a few inches
before those years
were shortened.
I've always wondered
how tall
the trees are now,
revolutions of the sun
sweeping us along
on our own waves
summer to winter,
winter to summer,
sunlight to darkness,
darkness to sunlight
as our bodies widen
and hair grays.
They must be giants by now
forming a wall
along the back edge
of the property.
Then I wondered
what if the new owners
removed them,
deleted the last shred
of us
from the patch

of ground
that passed to our hands
and imaginations
in the youth
of our dreams.
I decided to believe
they are still there,
sturdy, healthy,
forceful in their strength,
standing sentinels
for the new family,
watching for danger
like creeping apathy
and distrust
that poison the roots.
The trees
are still there
watching over
all of us
as the Sun
turns from one season
to another.

It Was Cold That Morning

Local paper,
birth announcements:

2:30 a.m. Monday morning,
to a teenage girl,
hindsight and alternatives.
The baby's father is listed as
Jack Daniels and insecurity.
Accompanying in the birthing room,
the girl's angry father
and her mother who won't look at the child.

4:37 a.m.
born to a childless couple
married 17 years,
a miracle.

6:38 a.m.
born to a scared woman of 32,
a son with the blond hair
of her lover.
Attended by her husband
whose life has suddenly become unbearable.

10:37 a.m.
to a drug addict,
a lifeless body.
She didn't make a sound

during the delivery,
she didn't say a word
as the child is taken away.

The parents of the morning go home,
never meeting one another,
but they all recall
how cold it was that morning.

The Call to War

Friday night 50°
a full star field in attendance,
a rush of voices fill the thin air,
steam from hot dogs, all beef,
floats into the chill,
delicate, perfumed hands
clap in rhythm, one, two,
in rhythm, three, four.
Boys at play
grass stains on the knees of their pants.

Friday evening 31°
a sky of silence.
Snow.
Falling on flesh and bone.
Rags covering dark skin
automatic weapons covering rags
automatic words covering the other side
where boys at war wait
for the halftime whistle.

Oblong, made of animal skin, floating in the air,
an abstraction,
until caught
by hands strong, but lacking in life,
confident in this moment
bathed in smiles and cheers and adulation
covering

the fear
of tomorrow. What of tomorrow
as the drums beat louder
in rhythm, one, two
in rhythm, three, four?
Grab your gear, move out
assembly point C, this is not a drill.

This is your day.
Picture in the paper,
kisses from the girls, oh
those kisses from the girls,
newspapers need to know
how did you do it,
how did you catch that pass?
Did you know

what had happened when
the explosion ripped through the compound?
Sergeant, can you tell us
how many dead?
How does this attack . . .
When were . . .
Why didn't you . . .
Should we bring our boys home?

Snow fell softly,
an afterthought to the cold.
The field is covered.
The stars gaze down
at a standing figure,
hands outstretched, waiting for the ball.
The clock ticks down.

The crowd is hushed,
anticipation a crafty thief.
Boy at play, holes in his pants,
cradles the pass, pulling it to his body
through his chest
and out his back.
The final whistle blows.

As Secret Writing Flourishes

The news plays in the background,
CNN talking heads 24 hours nonstop.

I hear about the bombs that went off
and the bombs that didn't.

4 a.m. and the pretty blond
is telling me the same things

that the pretty brunette told me
12 hours earlier.

4 a.m. and I still don't sleep,
three days and counting.

I watch the images
and read the headlines

but turn the sound down
so I can hear what remains

of your voice trapped
in the cracks of the plaster.

The Sun rises behind the house
while the overseas stock markets gain

and you tell me again
why I'm an asshole.

A fire in Cleveland rages out of control
while I wait for the apology

that always came, but this time
it sounds insincere

because your voice is fading,
the remnants too slender to register.

Your old letters are spread out
on the floor, trapping me

on the couch
so I don't step on them,

but I can't read your words anymore,
written in French or Gaelic

or some secret code.
What were you trying to tell me?

A man breathless and sweating,
speaking frantically

of his daughter wandering off
in a crowded Wal-Mart.

Under his impassioned face
CNN is trying to tell me something

with scrolling words
but I can't read them.

I pick up your letters
and I know

her name is Missy, and she's 4 years old.
I look at the TV screen

and it says
I am all you need.

Missy is wearing red shorts
and a white top.

You wish I understood
when you cry.

Missy was last seen
looking at the fish tanks.

It might be a mistake,
but you need to leave.

I drop your letters and turn off the TV,
sad realizations driving me.

If I find Missy
maybe I'll find you,

but I'm a thousand miles away
from Indiana

and if you were standing next to me
I wouldn't know where you were.

He Waited for the Carriage and Took Aim

The ship has run aground
and the ghosts
are getting off,
looking for home
and the peel of the welcoming bell.
Hollows and trails
are left in the black sand
by immigrant mothers,
moon-faced children and
men who would work for little,
and be remembered for nothing
until they fought
in the Great War.

It's quiet on the front
but for the echoes
of Princip's gunshot.

It's chaos on the front
except for the bodies
of the dead.

So we used the broad shoulders
of the survivors
to build the Great Society;
a chance for everyone,
a place for everything,
an answer to every question,
a woman for every man,

a father for every child,
a god for every faith,
until we asked
the sons of the settlers,
the next pioneers,
the young men,
to fight for it all again.

> Where do we start
> when there are so many
> who want it all?
>
> Flip a coin. Do you want
> to die in the jungle, the snow,
> or on a road into hell?

They came home
strong and proud.
They came home
on the same ships and planes
that brought home the dead,
came back with the same dreams
they had stored away
when they left,
and with our thanks fading
in the distance
like the voices of their friends,
they started a new life.
But at night
shades crept out of the darkness
stealing their breath and their sleep.
At night, the bedroom
became the jungle,

neighbors became faceless devils
with guns pointed at their heart,
and the world hadn't changed
despite the sacrifice.

South seas countries
we knew nothing about
at war with each other.

Why should we care?
Why should we go?
Why should we die?

The ghosts are going home,
tired of waiting
for us to wake up.
Their grandsons
and great granddaughters
keep up the fighting,
in caves and in deserts,
in speeches and in classrooms,
in elections and
at gravesides.
Gunshots fired
almost a century ago
have led us to countries
choosing up sides
for a playground game
that doesn't end with Mom
calling us home for supper.
Gunshots meant to secure
one country's freedom
have left us all shackled

to a sinking ship
and the ghosts
of the past
are tired of being ignored.

This Time

He waited.
One more sterile room,
one more chance
at either redemption
or a fourth opinion
the same as the first.
He waited,
vulnerable to the
homogenized air,
weak to the
betrayal of his body.
The skinned figures
on charts
stared back at him
with an accusing glare,
who is this interloper
into our world,
they whispered in strained voices
while the fabric
of the teal-green gown
kissed him all over
like his wife used to
before he became too fragile,
a porcelain doll
with a beard
and no appetite.
This time the news
will be good
he mumbled into the ether,

a soft nod
as back up confirmation.
This time the news
will be different
he tried to convince
the living man and woman
on the wall,
but they looked away
like old friends
who didn't know what to say.
This time, he thought
it has to be different.

Any of Them

He spun the globe
with a tired finger.

Something broke
in the background.

The countries blurred together
in a miasma of ink and imaginary lines.

Glass covered the kitchen floor,
and protruded from a child's foot.

His hand hovered over the globe,
deciding when to descend.

Screaming filled the house like water
while the mother tried to soothe.

He stopped the globe, Burkina Faso,
spun it again.

The glass came out,
cleanup began.

The globe slid under his finger,
South Bend, Indiana.

The mother is shouting his name
to come and help with the children.

He spun it so hard,
the blue and white sphere wobbled on its axis.

Mother shouting at him, pleading with the children,
children shouting at one another, pleading with him.

His index finger jabbed violently,
southern Portugal shuddered.

The injured child is running with fear,
trailing blood through the house.

His eyes cross painfully
watching the globe spin and spin.

"Why won't you help me?
Why are you just sitting there?"

Fictional borders disappear
into the greedy oceans.

Why is the TV on when no one is watching it,
why must the kids scream every word they say?

He doesn't stop it this time,
letting it choose for him.

The din becomes a hum
becomes an epoxy in the folds of his brain.

It stops under his pointing finger,
northern Pennsylvania, home.

Where did the quiet come from,
and why is it building in his ears?

He was pointing to his own house,
to his own beating heart.

He could feel them around him,
their voices fighting to get in.

He ended
where he started.

Acknowledgments

"He Fought" was originally published in *Another Sun* in 2002

"Beyond the Sunset" was originally published in *Rat's Ass Review* in 2021

"Afternoon Sky" was originally published in *Children, Churches and Daddies* in 2023

"Set List" was originally published in *Children, Churches and Daddies* in 2020

"Wretched" was originally published in *Eye on Life* in 2014

"S.O.S." was originally published in *Record Magazine* in 2018

"The Lonely Hours" was originally published in *Record Magazine* in 2019

"Saturdays" was originally published in the *Edged in Blue* chapbook in 2006

"Endless Clips of Ammo" was originally published in *Record Magazine* in 2020

"Days in the Past" was originally published in *Record Magazine* in 2021

"High Sun" was originally published in *Rat's Ass Review* in 2019

"North Carolina" was originally published in *Syzygy Literary Magazine* in 2015

"The Call to War" was originally published in *Ramble Underground* in 2006

"As Secret Writing Flourishes" was originally published in *Dead Snakes* in 2012

"He Waited for the Carriage and Took Aim" was originally published in *Eye on Life* in 2012

"This Time" was originally published in the *The Corrosion* chapbook in 2016

"Any of Them" was originally published in *Dead Snakes* in 2011

www.ingramcontent.com/pod-product-compliance
Lightning Source LLC
LaVergne TN
LVHW090050160826
845672LV00015B/1626

* 9 7 8 8 1 1 9 2 2 8 5 6 0 *